What was it like in the past...?

Clothes

Heinemann
LIBRARY

Kamini Khanduri

H www.heinemann.co.uk/library
Visit our website to find out more information about Heinemann Library books.

To order:
☎ Phone 44 (0) 1865 888066
🖹 Send a fax to 44 (0) 1865 314091
🖥 Visit the Heinemann Bookshop at www.heinemann.co.uk/library to browse our catalogue and order online.

First published in Great Britain by Heinemann Library, Halley Court, Jordan Hill, Oxford OX2 8EJ, a division of Reed Educational and Professional Publishing Ltd. Heinemann is a registered trademark of Reed Educational & Professional Publishing Ltd.

OXFORD MELBOURNE AUCKLAND JOHANNESBURG BLANTYRE
GABORONE IBADAN PORTSMOUTH (NH) USA CHICAGO

© Reed Educational and Professional Publishing Ltd 2003
The moral right of the proprietor has been asserted.

Designed by Celia Floyd
Originated by Ambassador Litho Ltd
Printed in China

ISBN 0 431 14821 X   (hardback)   ISBN 0 431 14831 7   (paperback)
ISBN 978 0 4311 4821 2   (hardback)   ISBN 978 0 4311 4831 1   (paperback)
07 06 05 04 03   08
10 9 8 7 6 5 4 3 2   10 9 8 7 6 5 4 3 2

British Library Cataloguing in Publication Data
Khanduri, Kamini
   Clothes. – (What was it like in the past?)
   1. Clothing and dress – History – Juvenile literature
   2. Costume – History – Juvenile literature
   I. Title
   391'.009

Acknowledgements
The Publishers would like to thank the following for permission to reproduce photographs:
Camera Press/Stewart Mark: 27; Camera Press/Terence Spencer: 22; Camera Press: 20, 29; Corbis: 23; Hulton Archive: 10, 11, 13, 14, 17, 24; Imagebank: 5; Mary Evans: 6, 8; Popperfoto: 4, 9, 18, 19; Powerstock Zefa: 26; Stone: 28; Topham: 7, 12, 15, 16, 21, 25.

Cover photograph reproduced with permission of Hulton Archive.

Our thanks to Stuart Copeman, and also Noreen Marshall at Bethnal Green Museum of Childhood for their help in the preparation of this book.

Every effort has been made to contact copyright holders of any material reproduced in this book. Any omissions will be rectified in subsequent printings if notice is given to the Publisher.

Contents

Words printed in **bold letters like these** are explained in the Glossary.

Each **decade** is highlighted on a timeline at the bottom of the page.

Then and now

Clothes have changed a lot over the last hundred years. Women's and children's clothes have changed more than men's have.

In the early 1900s, there were rules about what kind of clothes you could wear. Richer people had their clothes made for them. Other people bought ready-made clothes or made their own. Clothes were made from natural materials such as cotton, wool or silk.

This young boy was photographed in the 1900s. You can tell from his clothes that he comes from a fairly wealthy family. Many poor families could not afford to buy shoes for their children.

1920   1930   1940

Clothes today are often more comfortable than those worn in the past. Many clothes are now made from **synthetic** materials as well as natural ones. What material are your clothes made of? There may be a label inside that will tell you.

Today, girls and boys often wear the same kind of clothes.

1900s: Edwardian clothes

The 1900s are called Edwardian times after the king, Edward VII. A lot of women wore tight-fitting dresses with long skirts and long sleeves. Richer women had special dresses for the evenings.

Boys often wore sailor suits or jumpers and shorts. Most girls wore dresses. Both girls and boys wore hats and lace-up boots.

Most women wore corsets under their dresses to make their waists look smaller. It was hard to breathe properly in a tight corset and women often fainted.

Outdoors, women wore hats, held in place by hatpins. If it was sunny, they carried sunshades called parasols.

Businessmen wore either a suit, which was called a lounge suit, or a frock coat. Frock coats were sometimes slightly **flared** and were longer than ordinary suit jackets. They were worn with a shirt, trousers and a top hat.

'Children's hats are extremely dressy this season. They are frilly and fussy with laces and ribbons and adorned with daisies, forget-me-nots and other small blossoms...'
McCall's Magazine, 1908

1910s: Clothes for war and peace

Children's clothes did not change much during the 1910s. But women's clothes became a little more comfortable. Corsets were not as tight as they had been and dresses fitted more loosely over the body.

Some women wore skirts instead of dresses. Very narrow skirts came into fashion that were difficult to walk in. Women had to take very small steps so they did not split the **seams**.

*A French designer called Paul Poiret invented a fashion called the Oriental Look. Women wore satin **turbans**, and **tunics** over their dresses.*

1900   1910   1920   1930   1940

During the **First World War**, there were often shortages of material and people wore plain clothes. While men were away fighting, many women went out to work for the first time, in factories and on farms. Most women started wearing more **practical** clothes and some even wore trousers.

Special raincoats, called trench coats, were made for soldiers to wear in the muddy ditches called trenches on the battlefield.

1920s: Fun, freedom and flappers

After the war, women had more freedom. Younger women often wore more casual clothes such as looser-fitting dresses with shorter skirts. Short haircuts became fashionable too.

Women who wore the new fashions were known as flappers. Many young people started going out dancing to parties or dance halls.

These flappers are dancing the Charleston, a popular dance of the 1920s.

'My sister was a flapper… She always wore beautiful short dresses, fur coats, and of course – **galoshes.**'

Florence Arnold

There were school uniforms before this time but during the 1920s they became more popular.

Children's clothes were now made of softer materials. Boys started wearing shirts and shorts buttoned together into little suits. Girls still wore dresses.

1930s: Fashion and films

During the 1930s, lots of people lost their jobs and many had very little money to spend. One way to forget about the difficulties of real life was to go to the cinema. Films were a very popular type of entertainment in the 1930s.

Long skirts and dresses were fashionable for richer women at this time. Expensive materials, such as satin, fur and **crêpe de Chine**, were used.

Jean Harlow was a famous film star in the 1930s. The clothes and hairstyles worn by actors and actresses were copied by millions of people.

Before this time, women had always protected their skins from the sun and worn swimming costumes that covered up most of the body. Now sunbathing was popular and swimming costumes became smaller.

The first two-piece swimsuit appeared in the 1930s, though it was not called a bikini until the late 1940s.

1940s: Wartime clothes

During the **Second World War**, there were shortages of material, so clothes were rationed. This meant that each person could only buy a certain amount of clothing. Even babies' nappies were rationed. If you could not get enough you had to make do with other pieces of material.

This woman working in a factory is wearing overalls to protect her clothes and a scarf to keep her hair out of the way.

1940

People made their own clothes and, to use less material, most women started wearing shorter, knee-length skirts. Many women went out to work and wore **practical** clothes.

Many working women wore trousers as they were warmer and more practical than skirts.

Nylon stockings
Nylon stockings first appeared in 1939, but you could not buy them during the war. Women sometimes used make-up to draw a line down the back of their legs to look like a stocking **seam**.

1950s: Dressing up

In the 1950s, people could buy useful machines for their homes, such as vacuum cleaners. This meant that women with more money had more time to get dressed up and go out.

All kinds of dresses were fashionable. You could buy ball gowns, smart cocktail dresses and pretty summer dresses. What do you wear when you get dressed up?

Stiletto shoes first appeared in Italy in 1951. They had thin, high heels that got narrower towards the bottom.

Suits for women were also very popular. They were often worn with soft blouses and neat little hats. By the 1950s, more **synthetic** materials were being used and most women had stopped wearing corsets.

In the 1950s boys and girls started wearing trousers. They were either in **plaid** or plain material and often in bright colours.

This suit, designed by Coco Chanel, had a straight jacket and a narrow skirt.

1950s: Rock and roll

In the 1950s, some young men started wearing clothes based on Edwardian fashions from the early 1900s. They were known as Teddy boys. They wore their hair long at the back and brushed upwards at the front in a style called a quiff.

*Teddy boys often wore narrow trousers called drainpipe trousers, long jackets called frock coats, and shoes with **crêpe** soles.*

These people are jiving. Jiving was a type of dance often done to rock and roll music.

Teddy boys listened to rock and roll music, a type of dance music that began in the mid-1950s. It started in the USA but soon became popular everywhere.

The clothes and hairstyles of young people began to change to match those of their favourite pop stars. Teenagers also started to wear jeans at this time.

1960s: Miniskirts

In the 1960s, very short skirts called miniskirts were fashionable for women. At first people thought the skirts were shocking and they were only worn by teenage girls. Then women of all ages started wearing them.

Instead of girls copying their mothers' clothes, as they had before, it was the other way round. Do you wear the same kind of clothes as your parents?

Boots were often worn instead of shoes and tights were worn instead of stockings.

Clothes were colourful and often had bold patterns. New materials, such as plastic, were used for coats and boots. Children began to have more choice in what they wore and their clothes became more casual.

Small shops selling fashionable clothes for young people were called boutiques. This one was on Carnaby Street in London.

Mary Quant

Mary Quant was a very successful **designer** in the 1960s. She made cheap, fashionable clothes and make-up for teenage girls. Many people believe she invented miniskirts.

1960s: Clothes for men

In the mid-1960s, men began to wear more colourful clothes. They also started dressing more casually, instead of wearing shirts and ties all the time. Jeans became very popular.

The Beatles were the most famous pop group of the 1960s and lots of young men copied their clothes and their unusual haircuts. Is there a singer or pop group you like to copy?

The Beatles were known as the Moptops because of their floppy hairstyles. Sometimes they wore polo-necked sweaters with their suits, instead of shirts and ties.

1930   1940

Later in the 1960s, men called hippies grew their hair long and wore loose-fitting clothes. They often wore beads round their necks and sandals instead of shoes.

In the late 1960s, some people became hippies. Hippies were also called flower children.

1970s: Big flares and spiky hair

In the early 1970s, trousers called **flares** came into fashion. They were often worn with thick-soled shoes, called platform shoes, and sleeveless tops called tank tops.

Men, women and children began to wear similar clothes and long hair was fashionable for everyone. People also wore loose, flowing clothes, such as **kaftans** and **ponchos**.

Flared trousers could be very wide at the bottom and the soles of platform shoes were sometimes 17 cm thick.

Jeans were now worn by people of all ages and **denim** was also used to make things like jackets, skirts and bags.

Disco and punk rock were types of music in the late 1970s. Both made a difference to fashion.

Followers of punk fashion wore torn clothes, sometimes made of plastic, and often decorated with safety pins, zips or chains. They had spiky hair in different colours and both men and women wore crazy make-up.

1980s: Clothes for work and play

In the 1980s, unisex clothes (styles worn by both men and women) were popular. In the early 1980s, there was a kind of music and fashion called New Romantic. People dressed in showy, colourful clothes and some men wore make-up.

Also at this time, businesswomen started wearing suits to work. These suits looked like men's suits but usually had skirts rather than trousers.

The fashion for women to wear suits to work was known as power dressing. Women's shirts and jackets often had big pads sewn into the shoulders to make them look broader.

This was a time when many people had plenty of money and more free time than before. It became popular to keep fit by running, doing a sport or going to a gym. People wore sports clothes like tracksuits, T-shirts, sweatshirts and trainers. Do you wear clothes like this?

*Shellsuits were like tracksuits but were made of shiny, **synthetic** material. Sporty clothes like this were worn as everyday clothes too.*

1990s and 2000s: Today's clothes

Today, instead of everyone following the same 'look', people wear the clothes that they want. People dress more casually, even for work. Not many people make their own clothes.

Today, lots of children's clothes are made from fleece instead of wool.

Fleeces

Fleece is a new material made from plastic. It is often made from **recycled** plastic bottles. It is just as soft and warm as wool, but more comfortable to wear against your skin.

Clothes **designers** often get their ideas by looking at what people used to wear, so styles that were worn many years ago keep coming back into fashion. Often they have a more up-to-date look, or are made of different materials from the first time.

What do you think people will be wearing in the next hundred years?

Old styles often come back into fashion. Second-hand clothes shops can be a good place to buy them.

Find out for yourself

You can visit museums like the Victoria and Albert Museum in London, which has a large collection of clothes.

Ask your parents and grandparents if they have any photographs of the clothes they used to wear.

Books

History from photographs: Clothes and Uniforms, Hodder Wayland, 1999
Yesterday and today: What we wear, Franklin Watts, 2001

Websites

www.costumegallery.com
www.centuryinshoes.com
www.vintagevixen.com

Glossary

crêpe tough, crinkled rubber

crêpe de Chine silky material with a wrinkled surface

decade ten years

denim tough cotton material used to make jeans

designer person who makes original items, such as clothes

First World War when some countries including Britain, were at war with Germany, 1914-1918

flared/flares a piece of clothing, such as trousers, that become wider at the bottom

galoshes waterproof shoes worn over normal shoes to stop them getting wet

kaftan long, loose piece of clothing

plaid checked or tartan woollen material

poncho loose woollen cloak with a hole in the middle for a person's head

practical suitable for the occasion

recycled when something that is no longer useful is turned into something else

seam line where two edges are joined

Second World War when some countries including Britain, were at war with Germany, 1939-1945

synthetic made by people rather than being natural

tunic loose piece of clothing worn over a skirt or trousers

turban sort of hat made by winding a piece of material round the head

Index